HOW TO
Submit
TO YOUR HUSBAND
Joyfully

CASSANDRA ROBERTSON

CREATION HOUSE
A STRANG COMPANY

How to Submit to Your Husband Joyfully
By Cassandra Robertson
Published by Creation House
A Strang Company
600 Rinehart Road
Lake Mary, Florida 32746
www.strangbookgroup.com

This book or parts thereof may not be reproduced in any form, stored in a retrieval system, or transmitted in any form by any means—electronic, mechanical, photocopy, recording, or otherwise—without prior written permission of the publisher, except as provided by United States of America copyright law.

Unless otherwise noted, all Scripture quotations are from the King James Version of the Bible.

Scripture quotations marked AMP are from the Amplified Bible. Old Testament copyright © 1965, 1987 by the Zondervan Corporation. The Amplified New Testament copyright © 1954, 1958, 1987 by the Lockman Foundation. Used by permission.

All dictionary definitions have been quoted from Dictionary.com.

Design Director: Bill Johnson
Cover design by Nathan Morgan

Copyright © 2010 by Cassandra Robertson
All rights reserved

Library of Congress Control Number: 2010920442
International Standard Book Number: 978-1-61638-152-3
First Edition

10 11 12 13 14 — 9 8 7 6 5 4 3 2 1
Printed in the United States of America

To the many women whose lives will be changed by the contents of this book: look to God in all you do. He is faithful. Many of you have prayed for an answer to your marriage problem or your inconsiderate husband; here it is. Be open to what God is saying to you. My belief is that He will speak words to your specific situation that are not even contained in this book. That is how much He cares about what you are going through. God's desire is to see you whole in every area of your life, especially in your marriage. It is ordained by the Father Himself. God really loves you. He loved you enough to get this book to you. I know it will change your life. It has already changed mine.

Contents

Foreword

Letter to the Author

DEAR CASSANDRA,

Where do I begin? Even though we have only known each other for what some would refer to as a short period of time (four years), it seems as if I have known you forever. From the first time we spoke, there has been an unexplained connection that you and I have spoken about so many times.

When you called me and asked me to become such a special part of this wonderful blessing that you and your family have received, I was truly caught off guard but honored. This is truly a blessing, one so many people only dream about, and God could not have blessed anyone more deserving.

Upon receiving a copy of the book and reading the title, all I could do was laugh. God has a way of providing everything you need in so many ways when you are mature enough to receive it. I began reading it immediately and was able to recognize myself in so many ways. In the beginning of my marriage it was truly difficult to fully submit to my husband. Even though I loved him, some of the things that we were taught earlier in life always came to mind: always put a little money to the side just in case, never completely trust a man, all men cheat, etc. In other words, prepare for failure.

Not until my husband and I were invited to a service at

Faith Christian Center, Jacksonville, and started attending services regularly—being taught the Word of God and being able to understand it and make the necessary adjustments to live according to God's Word—did I even entertain the thought of truly being submitted and then receiving the true blessings that came and continue to come from it.

So often we try to have this conversation with women and share our testimony, and they are just not open to receive it. I feel as if this book is a tremendous tool that many women will be able to apply to help themselves as well as others. You have included a wealth of information for everyone to reference so that they can go to the Word of God and read it for themselves.

I guess we can add this book to our list of unexplained reasons why the connection between us has been so strong from the beginning. I thank God for giving you the wisdom, knowledge, strength, and patience to complete this book. It has truly been a blessing to me, as it will be to so many other women.

—Lesia Owensby
Jacksonville, Florida

Acknowledgments

T O MY WONDERFUL husband and children: Isidore, Areal, Isidore II, and Richard. Thank you for enduring my drastic mood swings during this project. You guys mean the world to me. I could not have been blessed with a better family with whom to share my life.

To my mother, Lillian, thank you for being my sounding board when I needed direction. Your input into my life is priceless. To my father, Richard, thank you for being a great example of what a true man is. You set the bar high as it relates to my standards in a husband. I had a wonderful childhood because of the sacrifices you and Mom made.

To my sister, Teresa, and my niece, Shaneka, thank you for giving me feedback and constructive criticism on my material. Your contributions mean a lot.

To my friend Lesia, a true example of excellence, thank you for praying with me, supporting me, and rejoicing with me. You are a great friend, and I love you.

Special thank you to Minister Trina Henderson.

Introduction

MANY WOMEN SUBMIT to their husbands because the Word of God says to, but they do not feel joy in their hearts from doing so. At one point I could definitely relate to those who feel that way. Because of my strong personality, submitting to my husband was one of the hardest things for me to do. I know I am not alone; that is why God instructed me to write this book.

During the process of writing I had been challenged more than I can ever express. So often I wanted to give up on this assignment, but the Spirit of God kept stepping in and pushing me to endure. I had to realize that it is not about me; the trials I endured in my marriage and during the writing of this book were for other women who may be dealing with similar issues. I have constantly stepped outside of myself to do exactly what is written in this book. Some days I was so overwhelmed that I didn't feel like I loved my husband. Other days I realized how much I love him and wondered what I would ever do without him. God is faithful; it got easier and it continues to get easier. If I had no struggles in my own marriage, how could I minister to other women who may be experiencing some of the same things? My experiences and God's faithfulness kept me going to show other wives how to submit to their husbands joyfully and with a pure heart. Many of you will find your answers as it relates to being a better wife from the contents in this book.

Believers can receive and relate to Jesus because He endured everything we can ever go through. The truth is, I would not be able to relate to the many women who are experiencing opposition in their marriages if my marriage had been perfect from the beginning.

This is a self-check book for you, ladies. My prayer is that you will finish this book a better mother, daughter, and sister, but most of all, a better wife.

one

What Do You Really Think About Your Husband?

WHY IS IT so hard for women to submit to their husbands? This is a question with many answers. Unfortunately for all of the women—saved and unsaved—trying to justify their behavior, none of the excuses are acceptable. God's Word is clear on submission; it is a direct commandment from the Father Himself.

> Wives, submit yourselves unto your own husbands, as unto the Lord.... Therefore as the church is subject unto Christ, so let the wives be to their own husbands in every thing.
>
> —EPHESIANS 5:22, 24

If you are struggling with submission, then you must question yourself as to whether you truly love God. Submission is not about you; it is about Him. Those who love the Lord keep His commandments.

> If you love me keep my commandments....He that
> hath my commandments, and keepeth them, he it is
> that loveth me, and he that loveth me shall be loved
> of my Father, and I will love him, and will manifest
> myself to him.

—John 14:15, 21

For years I was reading "submit to your own husband" in Ephesians 5:22 without really focusing on the last part of the verse, "as unto the Lord." You are pleasing God when you submit to your husband. Not wanting to submit to your own husband is not just an act of disobedience but also an act of selfishness and dishonor. How can you have such a problem with doing something as simple as submitting to your husband for God after all He has done for you? As you develop a closer relationship with God, it will become easier to please Him in the area of submission to your husband.

God desires for wives to submit to their husbands. It is absolutely amazing how many women disobey that command. How can you submit to your employer, pastor, police officers—who are likely somebody else's husband—and not submit to the one God called to take care of you and your children? Challenge yourself to do better in this area.

Men are totally different from women—how they respond to things, how they apologize; the list is endless. Men are not as thorough or consistent as women are, or at least that is what most women believe. Are our differences good or bad, and why did God make us that way? Well, think about this: our differences help us see the areas that need to be developed within ourselves. Unfortunately, instead of looking at our own flaws, we look at one another's faults and lose focus of what we need to ask G[...] fix in us. If we focused on our spouse's positive contributions [...] our relationships, our marriages would be considerably better. Sit down and really think about what attracted you to your husband, and write five or more outstanding qualities in your husband. After you write these things down, meditate on them. It will help you to keep a positive image of your husband in your heart.

1. his love for the Lord. His passion for the Lord.

2. The way he loves people as Christ.

3. He isn't selfish

4. He is madly in love with me.

5. He always is wanting the best for me.

If you can't think of anything good to say about your husband, what does that say about you? You married him; this should have been a breeze. Always look for the positive in your husband and

. Consistently build him up in the areas that
im. If you continue to build your husband
than willing to change in areas that you are
task should not be a guessing game. Get
ut and ask him what area he would like for
you to ~~~~~~, ~ y about. Then listen and receive what he says
without opposition.

As the head of the household, our husbands encounter more temptations and spiritual challenges than we do. The enemy thinks if he can knock the head of the household out, then the entire family will be destroyed. Well, he is wrong! Women are the keepers of the house, and it is our job to spiritually protect our husbands through prayer.

Opposition is very hard on a marriage. If you constantly oppose your husband when he opens up to you, he will eventually shut down. If your husband is complaining about something you are or are not doing, listen to him and make the necessary changes. Even if you disagree with what he is saying, think about this: you are looking at it from your perspective, not his. You can feel like the greatest wife in the world, but if your husband doesn't think so, discuss it with him and make the necessary adjustments. Remember, you are trying to please him. Oftentimes husbands don't communicate their desires effectively to their wives. If you are in this type of situation, go to God for instruction on how to take care of and pray for your husband. As a wife, you should have a submitted attitude in your marriage relationship, and your main focus should be to minister to your husband. Ask God to help you figure out your husband's specific needs, and be genuinely excited about making the changes Father God desires you to make concerning your husband. This will create unity in your marriage and at the same time make your husband feel important and worthy of your time and service to him.

PRIORITIZE

List your priorities in order of importance. List why you feel they should be in that order, and please be honest with yourself. Give Scripture references to explain why these things are in the order in which you have placed them.

Priority	Reason for This Order
1. _____	_____
2. _____	_____
3. _____	_____
4. _____	_____
5. _____	_____
6. _____	_____
7. _____	_____
8. _____	_____
9. _____	_____
10. _____	_____

Have You Validated Him?

What's your husband's worth, and are you willing to pay

With the sweet sound "I love you," with the
thoughtfulness of asking, "How was your day?"

With a special meal, or just building him up and letting
him know he is admired?

Stop nagging him about your honey-do list; the man has
been working hard. Girl, he is tired.

Get a nice, hot bubble bath ready with candles
surrounding the bathtub.

When he gets out of the water, give him a warm towel
from the dryer, or

Get the massage oil and give your man a nice body rub.

You say, "Yeah, right. That is impossible. I have to much
to do."

Now, would that be your attitude if it was him doing
this for you?

Not only will you make time for the evening, but you
will remind him throughout the day.

You will make arrangements for the kids, pets, and
dinner, even if you have to pay.

So why the attitude change when it comes down to doing
this for him?

Your friend needed a ride from work, your boss needed a
favor off the clock, and you had no problem catering
to them.

God gave you this precious gift to love, cherish, and to
take good care of;

To be a shoulder to lean and cry on, to show him
unconditional love.

Yeah, he may need a lot of work, but sweetheart, so do
you.

Maybe you should walk down memory lane and reflect
on all the things God has brought you through.

Be thankful for your true man of God. He is the priest
of your home.

Give your worries and concerns to Father God, the
mighty and majestic one who sits on the throne.

IT IS A BEAUTIFUL THING

Marriage is from God, and the Word says everything God made
is good.

> And God saw every thing that he had made, and,
> behold, it was very good. And the evening and the
> morning were the sixth day.
>
> —GENESIS 1:31

If we analyze ourselves instead of constantly analyzing our
husbands, our marriages will be happier, healthier, and they will
last longer. Why are wives missing the mark in this area? We
are missing it because we constantly look at our husband's faults
while overlooking our own shortcomings.

There is a reason that God made us different. If we were the
same as our husbands, what could we contribute to our relationships? As wives, we need to develop a desire to make our
husband's every waking moment wonderful, even if your husband

is not doing that for you right now. The Word of God says you reap what you sow. Eventually, if you continue to sow this type of positive behavior into your husband and your relationship, then you will reap the same type of positive behavior from your husband. Your marriage will be like heaven on Earth.

You can start sowing good seed now. Constantly build your husband up. Compliment him in his strong areas, and encourage him in his weak areas. Pay attention to your husband. If he feels tired, offer a massage, pay someone to do the yard. Think of creative ways to show your husband how much you care. Start the process of sowing good seed into your husband, and he will eventually follow and sow good seed into you. If you have been sowing bad seed, ask for a crop failure. God is faithful; He looks at our heart and responds accordingly. Develop a servant attitude as it relates to your husband; desire to totally please him. Your seed is powerful. Continue to water your good seed with positive confessions and the Word of God.

PRAYER CHANGES THINGS

Pray for your husband continually, especially when you are mad at him and don't want to. This does two things:

1. It calms your anger so you don't get out of hand and sin against your husband, and
2. It covers your husband in prayer, which is your spiritual duty.

The husband faces more temptations and trials because he is the head of the household. Satan comes after our husbands fiercely; he feels if he can take down the head of the family, the entire family will fall apart. In some circumstances, this may be true. This problem can be easily solved when a wife takes her role as the backbone of the family and keeps things functioning properly in her home through prayer. This is why constant prayer for our husbands is so important.

Temptations, for men, seemingly always come in the form of physical things. The very first temptation of man was in the Garden of Eden with something physical and good to look at. Sure, Eve gave Adam the fruit, but if it were not good to look at, would he have taken it? When Adam was created, he was given a command to take care of the natural things in the garden. He was to dress it and to keep it.

> And the LORD God took the man, and put him into
> the garden of Eden to dress it and to keep it.
> —GENESIS 2:15

Men are into physical and natural things. This started with the first man, Adam. Eve, on the other hand, had a spiritual relationship with God and her husband. There is no record of Eve doing any physical work in the garden. The last part of Genesis 2:22 says God brought her unto the man. Where did he bring her from? Maybe she was spending time with God and getting instruction on how to take care of His most precious creation. This may also be why women tend to be more spiritual. We notice spiritual things before we notice natural things. My husband used to always tell me to pay attention to my surroundings, and although that was good advice, I depended more on what I felt in my spirit and didn't really give much weight to my surroundings. I believe God taught women spiritual things first because God knew what the attack of the enemy on the family would consist of. God is faithful. He has already prepared women to handle any situation by taking it to Him in prayer.

Our jobs in the household are enormous and it can be overwhelming, but God has anointed us to do whatever needs to be done. We were made for the purpose of being a helper suitable for our husbands.

> And the LORD God said, It is not good that the man should be alone; I will make him an help meet for him.
>
> —GENESIS 2:18

Through prayer and meditation of the Word, God will show us how to effectively minister to our husbands, and He will show us how to maintain our joy during the process.

two

God Made Us Different for a Reason

IFFERENCES IN MARRIAGE can be really beneficial. For example, an affectionate wife can show a non-affectionate husband how important that aspect of a relationship is. The husband's and wife's differences can maximize the potential of one another in certain areas. Many people are convinced that life would be better if their spouse were more like them. If we were the same, life would be boring, and we would soon find out that we are not as wonderful as we think we are. The truth is, depression would be at an all-time high.

I used to expect my husband to do things the same way I would do them. I liked for the kids to get their bath as soon as they got home from school. My thought was that they had been outside the house all day. They were full of germs, so they needed a bath as soon as they get home. This would eliminate outside germs getting spread around the house, right? Well, to me that was a logical explanation, and it validated my belief.

My husband, on the other hand, preferred to let the kids wind down, relax a little, and then give them a bath before they went to bed. His way of doing things drove me nuts! I would come home and start multi-tasking like you wouldn't believe—

cooking, ironing clothes, trying to prepare lunch for the next day. I felt he could at least be doing some of the things that needed to be done. Watching my husband take a few moments to relax and get his thoughts together would always get me so frustrated that I would lose my temper and let him know that I did not need his help with anything.

After overworking myself, I had developed the worst attitude in human history. So now I was feeling exhausted, mistreated, mad, and ready to be joint-heir with my flesh. And he had better not even think about touching me later! All that drama, and, why, my husband never said he wouldn't help me; he just did not do it when or how I wanted him to.

The fact that your husband is totally different from you is OK. God made us that way. For many women, this revelation will eliminate a lot of frustration. After almost sixteen years of marriage, I finally got it, too. Now, instead of going through the same routine I have accepted the way my husband does things. I spent too much time being frustrated with him because he had his own way to get the job done. This unnecessary conflict can be avoided in our marriages if we accept the fact that it really is OK to be different!

THE BIG MISTAKES WE MAKE REGARDING OUR HUSBANDS

- Expecting him to do things the way we would do them.
- Expecting him to react to certain things as we would.

- Making decisions without consulting your husband first.
- Discussing personal issues about our relationship with family and/or friends.
- Constantly criticizing and tearing him down, especially in front of other people.
- Being a nag or complaining all the time.
- Not being willing to give him space or time for himself.
- Not being supportive of him or his ideas.
- Being unconcerned about his day or issues.
- Warring with in-laws when we as Christians should be the ones keeping peace.
- Never being satisfied, making him feel nothing he does is good enough.
- Embarrassing him in front of family, friends, or coworkers.
- Always looking for ways to prove him wrong.
- Wearing what others like to see you in and disregarding what your husband likes.
- Constantly denying him sex (without prior mutual consent).
- Making a spectacle of yourself. (You represent Christ first, then your husband.)
- Showing no respect for your husband or the people and things he respects.

WHAT DO YOU EXPECT FROM YOUR HUSBAND?

Are your expectations for your husband evident and clear to him? Women sometimes send mixed signals. We say one thing but express by our actions that we want something altogether different. For example, one Valentine's Day my husband asked me what I wanted. I said, "Nothing," and he didn't get me anything. I was furious! My husband's reasoning was, "You said don't get you anything, so I didn't." My reasoning was that he should have known that I did not want to pick my own gift but wanted him to get something from his heart. That year our Valentine's Day was horrible. I was really hurt and disappointed. Looking back at the situation, I can see where the confusion started: my expectation was not made clear. I expected my husband to know exactly what I wanted, but I did not communicate it clearly. Because of that I spent the entire day feeling hurt, unloved, mistreated, and irritated. I had all of these feelings as a result of my getting exactly what I asked my husband for—*nothing!*

You have to let your husband know what your requests are. Expecting your husband to be a mind reader will invite frustration and discontentment into your relationship. My husband did a lot of shopping for me in the beginning of our marriage. Like many couples, his taste and mine are totally different, and after years of irritation on both sides, now I do most of my own shopping. My husband became frustrated because I was always returning what he bought for me. He eventually decided to stop shopping for me. I became irritated because I thought after taking so many things back he would know my taste. I finally got the revelation that because I am trying to stay attractive for him, I should accept and wear proudly whatever he buys for me. Just recently he has started doing a little shopping for me again.

Another area where our requests should be made known is how we express our love for one another. I am a very affectionate person, so I was accustomed to showing my love through touching as well as verbally expressing my love. Isidore, my husband, expressed his love differently. He showed his love by buying me things, and he would always have new things for me. The differences in how we expressed our love to one another eventually became a major problem in our marriage. When I showed my love through affection, I expected him to show his love the same way. When he showed his love through giving gifts, he also expected me to show my love that way. I needed affection from him to feel loved, and he needed me to buy things to feel loved. There came a point when we both were dissatisfied in our marriage because he wasn't affectionate and I wasn't buying him anything. When we finally sat down and talked about it, we both discovered that we were trying to transfer our love style to one another instead of loving each other according to our unique needs. Once we realized that we expressed our love differently, the frustration ended because we learned one another's expectations.

The Word of God says with all your getting, get understanding.

> Wisdom is the principal thing; therefore get wisdom: and with all thy getting get understanding.
> —Proverbs 4:7

Communicate with your husband, and let him know exactly what you expect from him. Also, find out from your husband exactly what he expects from you.

Our differences add to our marriages. We must realize that they are good and capitalize on them. Your attitude about your husband's differences will determine if there will be a positive or negative outcome in your relationship. Be considerate and genuinely interested in making the differences between you and your husband work; use them to make your marriage better.

Nonverbal Ways Men Apologize

- Give gifts to you without it being a special occasion
- Be overly affectionate toward you
- Cook for you
- Wash the cars
- Finish the honey-do list
- Spring clean the way you like it done without you asking
- Help with all of the household chores
- Be at your beck and call
- "Yes" is the answer for anything you want to do
- Passionate lovemaking
- Spend more time with you
- Be extremely nice to you
- Things that they would not tolerate before for the moment seem to be OK
- Say and do things for you spontaneously

- Take you out to dinner to give you a break from cooking
- Be nice to family and friends they don't really like
- Call you during the day to hear your voice
- Give excessive compliments[1]

GIVE THE MAN SOMETHING GOOD TO LOOK AT

And God saw every thing that he had made, and, behold, it was very good.

—GENESIS 1:31

Your husband wants something good to look at. A large number of women, especially those who have been married for a long period of time, place little value on looking good for their own husbands. Everyone but your husband likes your hair, and you decide to go with the majority. Who are you trying to please and look good for if not your own husband? Your attitude should be that your husband is the majority; he should be the only one you are trying to appeal to.

Looking the way your husband wants you to look is a tough area because most husbands prefer a totally different style than their wives. For example, you may like silk or rayon and your husband may like linen or wool. Or maybe you like dark or neutral colors and your husband likes bright colors. So what do you do about this problem? Compromise, because if you only dress and do your hair the way you like it, how can you be totally attractive to your husband? Realize that men are visual.

---

1 This list was compiled through interviews with several men.

19

They respond to physical stimuli before emotional ones. This may be why Adam ate the fruit, because the Bible says, "It was pleasant to the eyes" (Gen. 3:6). You are your husband's trophy; he wants you to look good enough to show off.

Be flexible and willing to please your husband on every level. It will enhance your marriage greatly.

WHAT'S THE PROBLEM?

Making love to your husband is very important to him, and it should also be very important to you. One really big issue in marriage is women not being the initiator. Our husbands would love for us to be the aggressors. Many women feel like they don't have it in them, but we do have it in us. The first lady, Eve, proved that when she was the aggressor with the forbidden fruit. Eve is the female prototype.

How would you feel if your husband came home one day, cooked your favorite meal, gave the children a bath, and then catered to your every need without complaining? Or, what if he got up on Saturday morning and did all of the deep cleaning, washed, folded, and put away all the clothes without your asking? Can you imagine that? Think about how we would enjoy having a break from always doing most of the household chores. Put yourself in his shoes. He would love having a break from being the aggressor as it relates to making love. Lovemaking is just as important to our husbands as getting things done around the house is to us. Being the aggressor would be a huge ego-builder for your husband. Who wouldn't feel good about being wanted? For some women, it is going to take some effort, but this is a simple adjustment and it is possible.

Many women tire themselves out by taking on so many responsibilities, things such as cooking, cleaning, caring for the kids, and running household errands. But, we have to make it work for us. Prioritizing is key. For example, working women can get a head start by preparing meals on the weekend. Plan out a seven-day menu, wash and marinate your meat for the week, then seal it in freezer bags and put it in the freezer. Marinating your meat will save time, and you will not be sacrificing taste because the seasoning gets to soak into the meat. While you are getting dinner for the week ready, ask your husband to get your work clothes and the children's school clothes ready for the following week.

On Monday morning, move one bag of the meat you marinated from the freezer to the refrigerator before you go to work so it can thaw. When you get home, or even if your husband gets home first, all you have to do is pour the meat into a baking dish, cover it, and put it in the oven. Baking instead of frying is not only a healthier choice, but it also takes less time because you don't have to stand over the stove to cook. Multi-task while your dinner is in the oven. Most rice or side dishes have microwave instructions so you can have the side dish cooking in the microwave while the meat is in the oven. You can take your shower, bathe the kids, and fix lunches during this time, too; whatever needs to be done. Use paper products so you won't have to worry about a lot of dishes, or plan on using the dishwasher.

Your husband will appreciate this routine, and he will be glad to help because he will be getting a home-cooked meal every day of the week. Your husband will also notice and appreciate that you are not overworked and tired at night when it is his time.

For the stay-at-home mom, put your child or children on a

schedule. Your child's naptime is not the time to get things done; it should be naptime for you as well. Stay-at-home parenting is very demanding; there is always something to do. If you don't take time for yourself, you will never get time. A good tip, depending on the age of your child, is to let them help you with chores. Sing number songs or the alphabet while you work. This way you are bonding, they are learning numbers, letters, how to cook, and how to keep a clean house.

The bottom line is, once we learn how to prioritize, we can get things in order so we will have more energy. This will open the door for us to initiate the intimate action in our relationships, resulting in a very happy and smiling husband.

CHICKEN DIVINE

Recipe given by Alefia Wade

8 Boneless, skinless chicken breast strips
3 Tbsp. butter
2 c. shredded mozzarella or other Italian cheese
1 can cream of chicken soup
¾ c. white cooking wine
1 c. breadcrumbs

Preheat the oven to 425°.
Season chicken with salt, pepper, garlic powder, and paprika.
Melt the butter in a 9 by 13-inch baking dish.
Place the chicken in the dish and spread the shredded cheese on top of it.

In a separate bowl, mix the cream of chicken soup and the white cooking wine.

Pour the mixture over the chicken and cheese.

Sprinkle the breadcrumbs over everything.

Bake the chicken for 30–35 minutes.

Serve this dish with instant mashed potatoes or minute rice. Both of these side dishes are microwaveable. Pre-season your meat over the weekend.

IT DIDN'T WORK FOR EVE, EITHER

The Word of God makes it clear that one of the characteristics of the Holy Spirit is that He leads. Making decisions without our husbands is out of line; this area has been such a struggle for so many women, including myself. My bishop has been doing a series called "Extreme Makeover: Family Edition," and it has opened my eyes to so many things. Why are women always so tempted to make decisions without their husbands? The door was opened the day Eve decided not to include her husband in the decision to eat the forbidden fruit. Think about how many families have been divided and how many bad consequences have come to pass because of something as simple as a woman not including her husband in her decisions. Wives have to do better in this area; it is not God's desire for us to operate independently of one another. That is why God refers to husband and wife as one flesh.

> Therefore shall a man leave his father and his mother, and shall cleave unto his wife: and they shall be one flesh.
>
> —GENESIS 2:24

23

This certainly does not mean you should throw away your independent time; it just means that things concerning the both of you should not be directed by only one of you.

No More Excuses!

In many circumstances, good or bad, our husbands' actions dictate ours. This is not what God expects from us. Responding to all of our husbands' actions in a godly way is what pleases our Father in heaven. Reacting to negative actions is an expression of our flesh. Only the flesh feels obligated to respond; it convinces us that we will look like a sucker if we don't respond or that we have something to prove. Before you give in to your flesh, stop and think about who will get the glory with that behavior. It certainly will not be God. Slow down and get your thoughts together so you will not react to your emotions. Anytime an adverse situation arises in your marriage, you have an opportunity to grow up spiritually. Go to God in prayer and ask Him how to deal with the problem and how to have peace while going through the process.

The Bible says be quick to listen and slow to speak.

> Understand [this], my beloved brethren. Let every man be quick to hear [a ready listener], slow to speak, slow to take offense and to get angry.
>
> —James 1:19, AMP

Don't always be on the defensive when your husband is talking; listen to what your husband is saying. He may be talking out of frustration from having a bad day at work, or he may have misunderstood something you said and reacted out of offense. Remember what Proverbs 15:1 says:

> A soft answer turneth away wrath: but grievous words stir up anger.

Approach the situation gently; this will take prayer and obedience. The end result will be worth all of the effort you put forth in resolving this matter. The Bible says God sees what you do secretly and rewards you openly.

> So that your deeds of charity may be in secret; and your Father Who sees in secret will reward you openly.
>
> —MATTHEW 6:4, AMP

You are sowing good seed into your husband and you will reap the benefits of your obedience in the future.

In some situations, God will correct your husband through you, but only if you are mature enough spiritually and can correct him in love. When you choose to glorify God, you will see the situation continually get better.

We as women have to see the challenges of submitting to our husbands as spiritual opportunities. Spiritual opportunities help you to mature in the things of God. Anytime you plant good seeds and respond positively, you go higher spiritually. This will also keep the blessings flowing in your life. Because they depend on the choices you make, spiritual opportunities can also produce bad seeds, which will result in bad consequences. For example, if you and your husband get into a disagreement and no one wants to give in and apologize, you may decide to leave the matter unresolved. Because this matter is unresolved, strife has entered your house. The Word of God says confusion and every evil work come with strife (James 3:16). The bad consequences come in the form of "every evil work," and they have the right to be there because of strife. This could have been avoided in the beginning if you had taken the spiritual opportunity to grow, back down, and do what was right. Our husband's behavior is certainly not a justifiable excuse to act contrary to the Word of God. We all have to give an account of our own actions to our heavenly Father, and He is not going to accept the excuse "I did it because my husband made me by his actions."

First Peter 3:1–6 tells us exactly how we should win our husbands.

> Likewise, ye wives, be in subjection to your own husbands; that, if any obey not the word, they also may without the word be won by the conversation of the wives; While they behold your chaste conversation coupled with fear. Whose adorning let it not be that outward adorning of plaiting the hair, and of wearing of gold, or of putting on of apparel; But let it be the hidden man of the heart, in that which is not corruptible, even the ornament of a meek and quiet spirit, which is in the sight of God of great price. For after this manner in the old time the holy women also, who trusted in God, adorned themselves, being in subjection unto their own husbands: Even as Sara obeyed Abraham, calling him lord: whose daughters

ye are, as long as ye do well, and are not afraid with any amazement.

Meditating on this passage really opened my eyes and showed me that my words work much slower than my actions. You hinder what God is trying to do if you are constantly nagging your husband. For example, if the Holy Spirit is speaking to your husband and He is saying the same thing that you have been nagging your husband about, then your husband may be a little slower to obey because he thinks it is you giving the instruction and not the Holy Spirit. Stop talking so much; actions speak louder than words. Win him with your love walk. Many of you wives think it is going to take much more than a good love walk for your husband, but listen, God made the heavens and the earth; surely He can change your husband. Obey God where your husband is concerned and stop letting your feelings dictate the situation. God is a rewarder of those who diligently seek Him.

> But without faith it is impossible to please him: for he that cometh to God must believe that he is, and that he is a rewarder of them that diligently seek him.
>
> —HEBREWS 11:6

Your reward will come if you do your part. No more excuses, ladies!

three

God Is Speaking. Will You Obey?

I REMEMBER ONE SUNDAY morning my bishop was preaching a sermon titled "Don't Wait Until the Victory Is Over. Shout Now!" During this particular sermon God was dealing with me about being a better wife. Mediocrity had finally caught up with me. It was my choice to do the minimum; I was so convicted because I already knew I could do better.

I wanted to know what God expected from me as a wife, so I decided to devote my quiet time to getting in the Word of God and educating myself on what the Word says about wives. To my surprise, the only command I could find concerning wives was submit to and reverence your husband. I got really frustrated because I felt there was no instruction on how to be a better wife.

One day, I saw Beverly Juneau on television ministering about how wives should be treating their husbands. Isn't that like God? She said that our words are spirit and life, and she started explaining that the words we speak concerning our husbands enter into our spirits and produce life. You see, if you are always focusing on his faults and speaking of those things in him that you dislike, it will be a struggle for you to minister to him in love and with a good attitude. If you speak life into your spirit concerning your husband, no matter what the circumstances are, then eventually life will manifest itself in your heart and in your marriage. After getting that revelation, I started putting this principle to use in my life and God began revealing to me what kind of woman He desired me to be.

The Bible is very clear on what God expects from women. I believe words in the Bible that are referred to as "she" tell us His expectation. Proverbs 4:5–13 refers to wisdom and understanding as "she." James 1:4 calls patience "she." First Corinthians 13:4–5 refers to "she" as charitable, which means "long-suffering, kind, not envious, not puffed up, not boastful, behaves, not easily provoked, thinks no evil, not self-serving." Zion is the city of God, a permanent capital or monument (the word *monument* means "to guard, protect, and maintain"). Every woman living has the characteristics of guarding, protecting, and maintaining, especially if you are a mother or wife. The Bible also refer to Zion as "she"; could it be that when God gives the command for husbands to cleave to their wives (Gen. 2:24; Matt. 19:5) that He is really saying the same thing He said in Matthew 6:33: "But seek ye first the kingdom of God, and His righteousness; and all these things shall be added to you"? Husband and wife in God's eyes are one flesh; putting God first will always be beneficial to your marriage. Ephesians 5:22, 24 says we should be submissive. Proverbs 31:11 says we should be trustworthy. Proverbs 31:20 says we should be charitable and giving. Proverbs 31:25–26 says we should be honorable, strong, and kind. Proverbs 31:30 says we should fear the Lord. According to the Word of God a woman should be wise, understanding, patient, submissive, trustworthy, charitable, giving, honorable, strong, kind, fear the Lord, protectors, maintainers, guards, long-suffering, not envious, not puffed up, not boastful, not easily provoked, thinks no evil, not self-serving, and behaves. This list may seem long, but if you are walking with the True and Living God, think about it; you are already operating in most of these qualities. God has already equipped us with everything we need to take care of our husbands spiritually and physically.

Philippians 4:6 says, "Be careful for nothing; but in every thing by prayer and supplication with thanksgiving let your requests be made known unto God." Ask God to help you with the qualities that you don't have. Philippians 4:7 tells us that "The peace of God, which passeth all understanding, shall keep your hearts and minds through Christ Jesus." Trust God. He will never let you down. Philippians 4:13 says we can do all things through Christ who strengthens us. If you could not do it, the Word of God would not have said so.

Meditate on these scriptures and build your faith until you see a manifestation of what you asked Father God for.

YOU ARE THE APPLE OF GOD'S EYE

Wholeness is essential in effectively ministering to your husband. Many women are draining their husbands emotionally because they need constant affirmation to feel good about themselves. It is selfish to put that kind of pressure on your husband. There is a popular saying that two halves make a whole, but this is not true as it relates to believers. God created us whole. We are born with everything we need in life. Our circumstances and our environments are what change that.

If you constantly need to be complimented or constantly crave attention, you may have low self-esteem. Go to Father God for help. Self-esteem is something the enemy attacks on a regular basis. There are steps you can take to turning low self-esteem around.

- Ask God to help you with this issue.
- Find Scripture that explains what God says about you and confess it daily.
- Take godly pride in your appearance.
- Sow into someone else who may have low self-esteem. Help build him or her up.
- Compliment yourself. Don't wait for anyone else to do this for you.

It is important for you to go back and find out why you are experiencing these emotions. It may be something from your childhood that caused you to feel bad about yourself. Become accountable to someone else. Doing this will ensure that you stay focused on your goal of building your self-esteem. The more confidence you have in yourself, the more confidence people will have in you.

Our Father God is constantly building us up in the Scriptures. God said everything He made is good (Gen. 1:31). Proverbs 18:22 says he who finds a wife finds a good thing. God knew and approved of you before the foundation of the world. You are the apple of God's eye (Zech. 2:8). He sent His only Son to die for you and me! If God thinks so much of you, why is it such a struggle to think high of yourself?

SELF-ESTEEM CONFESSION

I am strong and of good courage because the Lord is
with me.

I am the apple of my Father God's eye, and therefore I
don't need man's approval.

I prosper in everything I do.

I am, according to the Word of God, wise,
understanding, patient, trustworthy, submissive, kind,
honorable, strong, long-suffering, not envious, and not
boastful.

I fear the Lord and honor Him in all I do.

I will walk with my head held high because God
approves of and knows me intimately.

I am an asset to my husband, my kids, and the body of
Christ.

I feel good about myself. I know my purpose, and I am
confident walking in it.

I will keep my appearance up and purpose to make my
inner person just as beautiful as my outer person.

I am a joy to be around because positivity surrounds me.

Thank You, Father God, for making it easy to be all that
You created me to be.

IT PLEASES GOD

Choosing to do what is right "every time" pleases God. It is so
easy to follow your flesh and act foolishly, but that would not be
pleasing to our Father in heaven.

Doing right when you are being wronged is a hard task, but if you maintain this discipline, you will keep going higher and higher spiritually. Some trials many women have faced are infidelity in their marriages or they are married to men who certainly make it hard to do right in the sight of the Lord. Even in those situations you have to take the high road and choose to act in a way that pleases God. Trials are really opportunities for spiritual growth, and it feels good to know that you have grown spiritually. The bottom line is you have to do what is right at all times; it will continually get easier, and pretty soon the enemy will abandon that way of temptation.

If you are in a situation that requires forgiveness, then forgive because it is the right thing to do; it is a commandment from God. Whether you choose to stay in the marriage is totally up to you, but do not feel condemned if that is your decision. If God is prompting you to stay in your marriage in spite of your husband's actions, obey Him and stand your ground, even when the negative crowd comes to give their opinion.

> Judge not, and ye shall not be judged: condemn not, and ye shall not be condemned: forgive, and ye shall be forgiven.
>
> —LUKE 6:37

> There is therefore now no condemnation to them which are in Christ Jesus, who walk not after the flesh, but after the Spirit.
>
> —ROMANS 8:1

Any negative feelings or feelings of guilt are not from God; they are from Satan. God has forgiven us for our years of unfaithfulness, and He is certainly not a fool. It is important for you to surround yourself with people who will give you godly counsel instead of merely offering their opinions. Too often we make decisions based on what other people think or on our emotions. God is not pleased with emotional decisions; they block our ears from hearing Him clearly.

There is a lesson in everything. If we stick around long enough, we will learn the lesson and have the joy and peace of God during the process.

FORGIVENESS IS ESSENTIAL

Forgetting the wrong that was done to you is something only God can help you with. Philippians 4:8 says we should think on things that are true, honest, just, pure, lovely, and of a good report. Infidelity does not fit this description, so don't focus on it. The enemy will keep the situation fresh. He will remind you every opportunity he gets. The Word of God says to take every thought captive. Meditate on Philippians 4:8 whenever the enemy attacks your mind with bad thoughts, and trust me, he will.

Most of us cheated on God for years, and He never turned His back on us. Why are we so quick to turn our backs on one another? By no means am I saying you should be a doormat or that God requires you to stay married after your husband has been unfaithful or abusive; each circumstance is different. However, if you decide to or have already terminated the relationship, make sure you do a heart check so that any bitterness or anger can be dealt with. Holding negative and unresolved feelings toward the person who hurt you stops your spiritual growth. Forgiveness is a commandment from God.

> For if ye forgive men their trespasses, your heavenly Father will also forgive you: But if ye forgive not men their trespasses, neither will your Father forgive your trespasses.
>
> —Matthew 6:14–15

We are made in the image and likeness of God. It should be easy to act more like Him. Unfortunately, that requires discipline and may require you to stop and actually think about your actions. The benefit of your discipline will result in you pleasing Father God by making better decisions.

How Do You Know You Trust God?

Trust God and you will be blessed.

> Blessed is that man that maketh the Lord his trust, and respecteth not the proud, nor such as turn aside to lies.
>
> —Psalm 40:4

It is human nature to be so self-sufficient; we exhaust every avenue before we go to the One who could have solved the problem in one step, with absolutely no frustration. If we were to look back, we would see how faithful God really is. The truth is, He has never let us down!

What are you doing that shows your trust in God? Not only

should there be corresponding actions for God, but there should also be evidence for others to see. When God fulfills His promises—and He will if the promise is in His Word—then that can help build someone else's faith, including your husband's. Trusting God takes patience, faith, temperance, and long-suffering. It is not an easy task at times, but it is rewarding.

God's Word is true, and it says He will never leave you or forsake you (Josh. 1:5; Heb. 13:5). Encourage yourself in the Lord. It is essential that you maintain your joy while you are trusting God because joy equals strength. Bad times come. They are a part of this life. How bad those times get depends on you. What will you say, or what will your words put into motion? James 3 lets us know how powerful our words are. The truth is, without bad times, how can the good times be appreciated?

You never go through trials without reason. When you are faced with tough times, you have to make tough decisions. When it is time to make those decisions, ask yourself, Is this about God or about me? Someone is always watching you and your demonstration of trust in God may be a testimony for others. God will take care of you as you take care of His business.

> But seek ye first the kingdom of God, and his righteousness; and all these things shall be added unto you.
>
> —MATTHEW 6:33

Things such as peace in your home, a loving and faithful husband, and a marriage that is like heaven on Earth are God's desire for us. If you are experiencing hard times in your marriage, instead of getting down and out or giving up, think of it as an opportunity to trust God. Focus your prayers on interceding for someone else's marriage, and watch God turn the bad situation in your marriage around. Job 42:10 says that when Job prayed for his friends, God restored Him. It's time to stop being so selfish and think about someone else.

> Know therefore that the LORD thy God, he is God, the faithful God, which keepeth covenant and mercy with them that love him and keep his commandments to a thousand generations.
>
> —DEUTERONOMY 7:9

That is an awesome promise from God; He has everything that concerns you on His mind. Meditate on Deuteronomy 7:9 when your situation seems impossible. Get a revelation that God had your problem solved before you knew there would be one. We serve a faithful God. Meditating on this verse will lift you up. Make a decision to let the Word of God be first place in your life. Even when things don't look like they are going to turn out for your good, trust God and let Him make the final decision in your situation.

TRUST GOD

Benefits of trusting God

- You will be blessed—Psalm 40:4
- He will direct your path—Proverbs 3:5–6
- He will defend you—Psalm 5:11
- He will keep you in perfect peace—Isaiah 26:3

- He will feed you and bring the desires of your heart to pass—Psalm 37:3–5

Our part

- Do good—Psalm 37:3
- Commit your way to the Lord—Psalm 37:5
- Offer up sacrifices of righteousness—Psalm 4:5
- Trust and take refuge in Him—Psalm 64:10, AMP
- Trust Him with all your heart, lean not to your own understanding—Proverbs 3:5

People who benefited from trusting God

- Gideon—Judges 7, 8:1–23
- Joshua at Jericho—Joshua 6
- Jairus—Mark 5:22–23, 35–42
- Abraham—Genesis 12:1–3, 22:1–18

There are certainly more benefits than this and more people who have benefited from God's faithfulness. Many of you already have testimonies of how God moved in your life when you trusted Him. For those of you who do not have a testimony, search the Scriptures and find your own examples. It will help to build your faith.

ACCOUNTABILITY IS GOOD

It is good to have a positive friend that you can trust. Get a married girlfriend you can fast and pray with concerning your marriage. Hold one another accountable to walk in love and speak life into your marriages. There are times you may get frustrated and want to give up, but your friend will encourage you to keep going. A breakthrough in either of your marriages will build your faith and help to motivate you. When you are in the midst of a situation, it is hard to see clearly. Your friend will be key to seeing the things you do not, and she will be key in ministering life into you. This will aid you in changing the situation.

Now, it is important not to get off balance. Your friend should not be making decisions for you but only positive suggestions. In an ideal situation, God will confirm things through your friend, things that you are dealing with and for which He has already given you an answer. However, if you and the friend you have chosen constantly disagree and offend one another, she is not the one to whom you should be accountable. And ladies, it is a very bad idea to make yourself accountable to a male friend. You will be putting yourself in an unhealthy situation, and you have to think about how your husband would feel.

Be prayerful about whom you should choose. God will lead you to the perfect person. Anytime we have a need in our life, God faithfully provides the seed. All you have to do is ask. God will send you someone with the same marital issues, someone you can relate to and fervently pray for.

four

What Kind of Woman Are You, Wise or Foolish?

Every wise woman builds her house, but the foolish one tears it down with her own hands.
—Proverbs 14:1

TEN KEYS TO BUILD UP YOUR HOUSE

1. Submit, subject (Prov. 12:1; Eph. 5:21–23)

God's Word doesn't say you should submit to your husband only if he is saved, but it does say to submit to him as unto the Lord or in the fear of God. This means that when you submit to your husband you are honoring God and showing respect to Him.

2. Consult with your husband before making decisions (Gen. 3:1–6).

Eve got us all in trouble by making this mistake.

3. Take responsibility for your actions and stop blaming others (Gen. 3:13).

Don't let your husband's actions dictate yours.

4. Desire your own husband (Gen. 3:16).

5. Lose the attitude (1 Pet. 3:1–6).

Stop putting more time into your appearance than into the transformation of your attitude. If you are not putting time into either of them, shame on you!

6. Thank God for your husband (Eph. 5:20).

What you say about your husband gets in your Spirit (Ps. 119:130)

7. Don't use sex as a tool or revenge (1 Cor. 7:4–5).

8. Be trustworthy (Prov. 31:11).

Your husband should be able to trust you in everything.

9. Treat him the way you want to be treated (Prov. 31:12, 26).

No matter what he is doing, you are accountable to God for your own actions!

10. Ask God to show you exactly what your husband needs (James 1:5–8).

It may look bad now, but nothing is too hard for God (Jer. 32:17, 27). Maintain your confession, no matter how the situation looks. Believe God will do it (Num. 23:19)! And remember, you can do all things through Jesus. He is your strength (Phil. 4:13).

You are now accountable for everything you have read and heard (Eccles. 1:18).

THINK ABOUT IT BEFORE YOU SAY IT

It is very important to control your tongue when you are angry. Proverbs 15:1 says a soft answer turns away wrath, and grievous words stir up anger. Proverbs 15:2 says, "The tongue of the wise useth knowledge aright: but the mouth of fools poureth out foolishness." Sarcasm is never good. You should respond in love to your husband at all times—on purpose. It may not always be easy to do this, but it will be very rewarding. Eventually the situation will change for the better, and you will have grown spiritually in the process.

What you say about your husband and what you say to your husband take form in your heart. For example, if you constantly put your husband down, you are developing that image in your heart, as well as in your husband, and eventually he will become whatever you are labeling him.

> Every wise woman buildeth her house: but the foolish plucketh it down with her hands.
>
> —PROVERBS 14:1

Whom do you identify with? You should identify with the wise woman. Build your husband up. Let him know how proud you are of his commitment to the things of God. Tell your husband how much you appreciate his contribution to the family. Do special meals or make random phone calls to see how he is doing. Let him know he is loved and appreciated.

Control Your Tongue

Why is it so hard to control your tongue?

Would submission be easier if you just did not have one?

So, he made you angry and now he is getting the silent treatment because you don't want to talk.

Is this what Jesus would do? What about your love walk?

Control your tongue when you are angry and try not to say a mean word.

Be a doer of the scriptures and apply what you have read and what you have heard.

If you submit to your husband as unto the Lord, peace will be in your house. Joy will abound.

Honoring your husband will ensure that love and happiness will always be around.

Before you speak out in anger, stop to think of the effect.

Stop to think of the consequences, which will be strife, hurt, and you both feeling neglect.

Go into your prayer closet and ask Father God in heaven to handle the situation.

Ask Him to take away the results of your restraint, which are hurt and feelings of frustration.

Put your trust in God, and eventually it will get easier and not be so hard.

And then you and your husband can rest easier and not have to always have up your guard.

Give your worries to our Father in heaven. He will exchange it with His best.

Do not be heavy-laden. Just dwell in God, and He will give you some much-needed rest!

BE YE ANGRY, BUT SIN NOT!

When your husband pushes you to your limit, it is OK to get angry, but don't give in to your flesh. The Word of God says:

> Be ye angry, and sin not: let not the sun go down upon your wrath.
>
> —EPHESIANS 4:26

What is sin? Dictionary.com defines *sin* as "deliberate disobedience to the known will of God."

It is important for you to search the Scriptures to find out what God expects from you as a helper suitable for your husband. Ephesians 4:29 says, "Let no corrupt communication proceed out of your mouth," so cursing your husband when you get mad at him is sin. Ephesians 4:29 also states that communication should edify and "minister grace unto the hearers." Calling your husband stupid or any other mean name you can think of is sin. First Corinthians 7:4–5 states the wife doesn't have power over her body, but the husband; it also states the opposite is true. When verse 5 says, "Defraud ye not one another." Withholding sex from your husband is sin. First Peter 3:1–6 tells you to win your husband with your conversation and "the hidden man of the heart." Walking around with a bad attitude and not speaking to your husband is sin. A bad attitude hurts you, especially in your marriage; it is like a repellant that pushes people away.

We will at some point reap what we sow into our husbands. If you continue to honor God by submitting to your husband, He will show Himself to be faithful and will reward you openly.

Totally submitting to your husband is pleasing to God. You are not wrestling against flesh and blood.

> For we wrestle not against flesh and blood, but against principalities, against powers, against the rulers of the darkness of this world, against spiritual wickedness in high places.
>
> —Ephesians 6:12

Every battle you have is spiritual. The good news is, it is not your fight. It is the Lord's.

> And he said, Hearken ye, all Judah, and ye inhabitants of Jerusalem, and thou king Jehoshaphat, Thus saith the Lord unto you, Be not afraid nor dismayed by reason of this great multitude; for the battle is not yours, but God's.
>
> —2 Chronicles 20:15

WHERE TWO OR MORE AGREE

The power of agreement is phenomenal; that is why the enemy constantly attacks marriages. When a husband and wife come into agreement through prayer with one another, they get exactly what they pray for. Can you imagine how many mountains would be in the sea if husbands and wives came into agreement on a regular basis?

Genesis 11:1–6 gives an example of the power of agreement. Those people could have built a ladder to heaven if God had not confused their language. The results of unity make it essential to keep peace at all cost. You may be tired of being the peacemaker, but remember, you reap what you sow. Soon you and your husband both will be peacemakers and in total agreement. This principle will also work for the women with unsaved husbands.

The Word of God says "two or more in agreement," it does not specify who the two or more should be. You can be in agreement with your Spirit-filled girlfriend until your husband comes around. Meditate on 1 John 5:14–15:

> And this is the confidence that we have in him, that, if we ask any thing according to his will, he heareth us: And if we know that he hear us, whatsoever we ask, we know that we have the petitions that we desired of him.

It will reassure you that God hears your prayers and desires to answer them if they are in His will.

Jesus Is

Jesus is our Rock, the Source of our salvation.
Jesus died for our sins, He earned His exaltation.
Our lifestyle should fall in line and be pleasing to Father God.
Living upright and holy is enjoyable and really not that hard.
Get a revelation of the benefits of His death for you and for me.
He gave us the world and the fullness thereof; what more do we need to see?

Exceedingly, abundantly blessed above all we could ask or think,

God does not need us; we need Him, because we are the weakest link.

The Bible is clear when it tells us about the power of our words.

The Bible is also clear about the battle not being ours, but the battle being the Lord's.

So why sit around complaining like Job and magnify our frustration?

God gave us authority; our lack of results is because of our own procrastination.

Our life is a result of what we have been doing and what we have been saying.

Why are we angry at God, when we are the ones who are not obeying?

Believers are joint heirs with Jesus, righteous by association.

We should be thankful beyond measure, expressed by our demonstration!

ALL YOU HAVE TO DO IS ASK

We are joint heirs with Jesus (Galatians 3:29; Titus 3:7; James 2:5). Jesus got results, and so should we. There are too many women struggling with getting results in their marriages. Can it be because they do not have confidence in their prayers? God loves you so much, and His desire is to see you happy. Romans 8:32 says that Father God "spared not his own Son." Think about this: if God gave Jesus, His only Son, why wouldn't He give you what you are asking for? As long as our requests are in line with God's Word, we can have it.

There are numerous scriptures telling us just to ask. Here's one:

> And I say unto you, Ask, and it shall be given you; seek, and ye shall find; knock, and it shall be opened unto you.
>
> —Luke 11:9

Waiting may be the hard part, but James 1:4 says, "Let patience have her perfect work." The end of that verse says if we do this, we will be "entire, wanting nothing." God is never the problem; His timing is perfect. We are the ones who constantly get in the way with our solutions.

There have been many things I asked God for over the years, and looking back I can truly say I was not ready to receive those things. It is funny to think about the season I was in and how convinced I was at the time that I really was ready. If Father God had granted my request, I would have really messed my life up. Can you examine yourself and say that you are really ready for the request you have made before God? Be honest with yourself. Make a list of your requests. Answer yes or no if you are ready, and then put why. Here is an example:

Request	Are you ready?	Why are you ready?
Financial Breakthrough	Yes	We are faithful tithers and we desire to bless others as well as finance the kingdom of God.
Change my husband	No	I am not willing to change.

Most married women have a request before God to change their husbands but are not willing to change themselves. I noticed every time I yielded myself to God and allowed Him to change me, my husband changed also, without my saying a word.

Women can be responders (allowing our actions to be dictated by our husband's), and many times we develop bad behaviors in response to our husband's behavior. The Word of God is clear on our being accountable for our own actions, so we have to change our own behavior on purpose and stop worrying about our husbands. If you turn your husband over to God, God will work it out. This is certainly not an easy task; I am still being worked on in this area. Ask Father God to show you what needs to be changed in you. He is faithful. Remember, you will reap change if you sow change.

CHANGE IS GOOD!

Your Change	His Response
I stopped nagging him about church and had an extremely good attitude after service.	He started asking me about the message and eventually asked if he could come with me.

Your Change	His Response

THE BEST MEDICINE

Marriage is very challenging at times. It is vitally important to seek God at your low points. He is faithful to bring you out of any situation. The best medicine is seeking God in the rough times. This is an area you have to really be disciplined in because the flesh always has a solution. I am sorry to say that I did not always make the right choices when things got rough in my marriage, but when I finally did go to God and His Word, He gave me peace during the process of working things out.

God is so good about encouraging you when you are going through rough times. If I turned to TBN when I was struggling, there was always a sermon on that would be exactly about what I was dealing with, and there would be a solution. When I felt sad, my son would call home from college and share funny stories with me. Every single time I was sad, God would have him call. When I didn't feel love, my two younger kids seemed extra affectionate. If I just sat and meditated on my hurt, the phone would ring, and it would be one of my married girlfriends needing encouragement. That would always get my mind off of my problem. When you encourage someone else, the Holy Spirit ministers to you as He is ministering to the other person through you.

God is faithful in all things. If you trust Him He will do exactly what you ask if it lines up with His written Word. God's desire is for us to do good, to be good, and to have everything that is good. He is no respector of persons: "For there is no respect of persons with God" (Rom. 2:11). God keeps me, and if you trust Him, He will keep you as well.

BE STILL AND KNOW HE IS GOD

When you are standing and believing God for something, the silent times are the hardest, but they are also the most effective. Silent times work on you as well as your situation when you bring them before the throne of God.

There may be times when you have to sit back and watch your husband make bad decisions and not react to them. In my marriage, I was always voicing my opinion. I just needed to let my husband know how bad I thought his decision was. I thought that would help him to see things clearer and make better decisions. Instead, what my input did was slow the process because he was confusing God's voice with mine. Wives have to learn when to be silent. If God does speak the same thing to your husband that you did, he may not obey because your husband may not be clear if it is your words he hears or God's. Also, keep up your guard as you pray for your husband, because the enemy will make sure you have plenty of opportunities to make a bad decision yourself.

Be still. Why do you have to be heard? What is your motive? Nagging your husband about any situation causes your husband to rebel, and your husband's rebellion toward you hinders his prayers from being heard by God.

> Likewise, ye husbands, dwell with them according to knowledge, giving honour unto the wife, as unto the weaker vessel, and as being heirs together of the grace of life; that your prayers be not hindered.
>
> —1 PETER 3:7

Wives have a major part to play in this particular verse. Make things easier by being a helper suitable for your husband.

God's timing is perfect. If you cannot handle the waiting process, stop wasting God's time as it relates to changing your husband. If your husband's bad decision is putting your family in danger, then naturally, you must take immediate action. But if your husband's bad decision is not putting the family in any type of danger, then you need to sit back and let God work. God will reward you for doing things His way. At some point your husband will acknowledge that he should have listened to you after all. Your husband will eventually value and even ask for your opinion. Intercede for him. *The Power of a Praying Wife* by Stormie Omartian is an excellent book. Every married woman should have a copy.

five

Ten Things Every Woman of God Should Be

1. *Praiseful*: Blesses, harvests, celebrates, expresses thanks, is thankful, is a worshiper

2. *Prayerful*: Intercedes, seeks and asks, requests, calls, invites

3. *Poised*: Assured, confident, composed, holds balance, stands in readiness

4. *Playful*: Pleases, amuses, laughs, plays

5. *Progressive*: Moves forward, advances, continues steadily by increments

6. *Persistent*: Refuses to give up or let go, insistently repetitive, endures

7. *Patient*: Mild, gentle, bears trials

8. *Peaceable*: Still, undisturbed, a peacemaker

9. *Perceiver*: Understands, discerns, becomes fully acquainted with, observes fully

10. *Prosperous*: Able to capitalize, successful, flourishes, favorable, well off

Praising is very important in the life of a woman of God. It is especially important for wives because we are the intercessors for our household; we need to maintain a special connection with God. The benefits of praise are endless. More importantly, it establishes an intimate relationship with our Father God. Praise is one way we can give back to God, and spending time in the presence of God makes you familiar with His voice and His ways.

Because our husbands face far more temptation than we do, it is our spiritual responsibility to keep them covered in prayer. Being *prayerful* is vital in the life of a woman of God. The Bible says the man is the head of the woman, so the enemy figures if he can take the man out, then everyone else will fall. The devil is a liar. True women of God are the backbones of their households. God has equipped us with everything we need to take care of our families spiritually.

Loosen up and be *playful.* The Word of God says, "The joy of the LORD is your strength" (Neh. 8:10). You are not more anointed when you are serious. It is no fun being around a person who analyzes everything and makes no room for fun. You can break so many chains if you just loosen up, enjoy God, and enjoy the life He has blessed you with. My husband, kids, and I get together and play games and laugh. We just enjoy each other's company. Most of the time my daughter and I start the fun. The tone of the woman often sets the tone for everyone. Help your family members maintain their joy and strength in the Lord.

Why waste time on something that will not push you forward or higher? *Progression* is essential to the plan and purpose of

God for your life. Your spiritual progression is not just for you. God puts people in our paths who need the anointing He has blessed us with. Jesus was our example; He died on the cross for us. Because of His death, He has the name above every name, and we benefited by inheriting eternal life. When Jesus made a decision to progress, He set a pattern for us here on Earth. Wives are the examples in the home. If our husbands and our kids see us progress in the things of God, then they will be motivated to do the same. God's Word says we should seek the kingdom first (Matt. 6:33). Spiritual progression in the life of a believer is very important. Progression is a benefit of making God and His Word first place in your life. Make God first, and progression will be easy.

Women of God should be *prosperous*. God has given every person gifts and talents for us to use, and we should apply them in our lives. Some of you have had God-ideas forever, but what good will they do if they are not implemented? God gives us the power to get wealth. He does exceedingly and abundantly above all we can ask or think according to the power that *works in us*. (Eph. 3:10) The power is the Holy Spirit. If we will take the first step, He will lead and guide us into all truth. You will not need a market analysis to know what to do. The Holy Spirit will show you exactly how to tap into the riches of this world. Pray and ask God to show you what He desires for you to do with the money. Once we tap into the wealth, we have to be faithful to help finance the gospel. Wealth is for making sure the good news gets preached to every creature. Do not worry about the stuff. God is faithful. He will make sure you get the desires of your heart.

Stay *poised,* woman of God. Keep your composure. The Word says, "In due season we will reap, if we faint not" (Gal. 6:9). It also tells us to stand fast in the freedom that Christ has given us and to "be not entangled again with the yoke of bondage" (Gal. 5:1). The easiest thing to do in a tough situation is to give into your flesh, but that is contrary to the Word of God. Keeping your composure will help you to be still and wait on God. Ask Him to help you get through your situation. Listen intently and obey quickly.

So many good things come out of being patient. *Patience* is one of the most valuable assets a woman of God can have. It is so easy for the enemy to attack in this area because our attitude is, "We want it, and we want it now." Having patience does not mean the answer is no; it means understanding that the timing just is not right. The Word of God calls patience's work "perfect," and it says it will make us "perfect and entire, wanting nothing" (James 1:4). God uses patience to perfect in us the things that we need to go to the next spiritual level.

Persistence is very important in the life of a woman of God. We must persistently pray for our husband, children, and one another. A perfect example of persistence was the woman with the issue of blood (Matt. 9:20–22). This woman was persistent in her faith for twelve years, and because of it she was made whole.

> Blessed are the *peacemakers:* for they shall be called
> the children of God
> —Matthew 5:9, emphasis added

We women have the tremendous task of keeping everyone in the house happy. Maintaining a peaceful atmosphere at your home is certainly a good way to start. Our husbands are still carrying out the call given to Adam of dressing and keeping the garden; you were a part of the garden. Providing for their family with all of the opposition they face is a tremendous task. Most husbands want to be good providers. Unfortunately, some incomes do not allow it. Maintaining a peaceful atmosphere at home will help keep your husband's stress level down and will keep peace and happiness in your marriage as well.

We must *protect* our family through prayer. Prayer is essential to the protection of the people we love most. We are the vessels God chose to be stewards over the people we love; our husband and children belong to God. This is quite an assignment, but you are already equipped with everything you need to get the job done. God has given all who have accepted Jesus the gift of praying in tongues. Tongues is your own personal language, spoken directly to God.

> For he that speaketh in an unknown tongue speaketh not unto men, but unto God: for no man understandeth him; howbeit in the spirit he speaketh mysteries.
>
> —1 Corinthians 14:2

Your own personal prayer language has many benefits, and through prayer, God will let you know everything going on with your loved ones. As we go before Father God praying for our loved ones in tongues, the Holy Spirit is making intercession. The perfect prayer is being spoken in the heavenlies by us via the Holy Spirit. There is no protection greater than our God, so we should take advantage of this powerful gift.

For Single Ladies

Don't act single if you are believing God for a mate. Act married. Maybe you're wondering, "What does she mean by that?"

That does not mean cook and clean for or make love to the person you are dating. Making love is only authorized in the context of marriage. God will not be pleased with you making the decision to violate His temple. Your body is the temple of God and should be kept holy and acceptable unto God (Rom. 12:1). Jesus made that evident when He knocked over all the tables in the synagogue because it was made into a den of thieves. He was not pleased with the violation of the temple. Cooking, cleaning, and washing clothes for your man are benefits of marriage and should be withheld also. If you give your all before marriage, what will you have to offer after you guys say, "I do"? That is how most men think. Why would they make a binding commitment to something they can sample freely? If your guy is pressuring you for any of these things, that shows lack of respect and likely means he is not the one God has chosen for you. Your sacrifice and honor should be to God alone until you are married.

The way to prepare for marriage is to develop a routine. Cook on a regular basis, even if it is just for you. Take a certain amount of time every day outside of your time with God to minister and be a blessing to someone else, maybe a niece or nephew or even a good girlfriend. You can also visit a homeless shelter to volunteer. When you do get married, this will help you to be accustomed to setting time aside for your husband. Many married women let the tasks they have as a wife cut into their husband's time, but you don't have to make that mistake.

Start speaking in line with what you want in your husband and be willing to be all of those things yourself. Being single gives you a lot of time to work on you. Many women ask God to instill qualities in their husbands that they do not have themselves. Many single ladies have developed bad habits, and their attitude may have come from being single and doing things their way for so long. Ask God to show you the areas in which you are selfish and not willing to compromise. Then ask Him to show you how to change this attitude. First Peter 3:1 tells women to win their husband over by their inner person. This is the most important aspect of winning your future husband or fiancé. Finally, don't discount your appearance. It matters also. Keep your appearance tight.

IT IS ALL ABOUT HIM!

Behold a handcrafted, beautiful, and strong vessel made by God Himself,

Created with perfect precision, birthed in a garden of wealth.

But still you are acting desperate and letting guys not after God's heart hang around.

Here is a simple but effective prayer: ask God to freeze it from the waist down.

How can you disrespect Father God by constantly settling for less?

He is not pleased with that. God sent Jesus to show you He wants you to have His very best.

The Scriptures say you will be in perfect peace if your mind stays on God,

But your mind is on everything but Him. You are the one making this journey long and hard.

Have you considered that you have not received what you have prayed for because God is still working on you?

Be patient, focus on Him, and Father God will bring you through.

You're pursuing the man that you think is the one, and that is totally out of order.

Acknowledge the Word of God; He needs to find you; remember you are the Most High's daughter.

So single ladies, put your focus on God in all that you say and do.

He is not withholding any good thing; He and the good things are at the finish line waiting on you!

Ruth Did It. So Can You.

Dealing with your husband's family can be challenging, especially if they are not Christians. It is not your responsibility to correct your in-laws. It is the responsibility of your husband as the man and priest of your home. Conflict with your in-laws is a sensitive area in marriage and can really cause a lot of strain in your marital relationship. Many wives feel that their husbands are passive as it relates to dealing with issues concerning their own families, and in some cases that may be true. If the way your husband chooses to deal with the situation does not solve the problem, then take it to God.

The Word of God says love never fails (1 Cor. 13:8), so that should be your starting point. Show your in-laws unconditional love by mimicking the way Jesus treated people. The perfect example of love is the way Jesus responded to the people who crucified Him. They whipped Him until His flesh was torn off. They pierced His side. They spat on Him. They mocked Him. The list goes on. Nevertheless, Jesus responded by praying for them to the Father. Jesus did not address the people who crucified Him; He addressed God as He prayed for them. Addressing your in-laws inappropriately will just cause strife, which will open the door for confusion and every evil work.

> For where envying and strife is, there is confusion
> and every evil work.
>
> —JAMES 3:16

We have to remember that we have not always been the most loveable people to deal with. Our choice to forget our past might make us think we can judge others, but it is not so. Seek God aggressively concerning your in-laws. He will instruct you on how to deal with them! Different people have different understandings of what it means to love. Ask God to show you exactly how to minister to your husband's family in their love language.

FOOD FOR THOUGHT

- Do you have a short temper when it comes to your husband?
- Does he constantly get on your last nerve?
- Are you turned off by him? If yes, why?
- Are most of your thoughts and feelings about your husband negative?

What Are You Thinking About?

Philippians 4:8 says think on things that are true, honest, just, pure, lovely, and of good report. If your thoughts do not meet all of these requirements, then you should not be thinking them.

Meditate on This

- How did he ask you to marry him?
- What was your most memorable gift from your husband?
- What did he do to let you know that his love for you is unconditional?
- What is the nicest thing he has ever said to you or about you?
- How well does he provide for you?
- How intelligent is he?
- Is he a good father?
- Think about the good times you have together.

I'm sure you have a lot of wonderful memories you can add to the list. The point is for you to think on the good things. If your words are in line with God's Word, everything good you confess about your husband will come to pass.

Conclusion

I PRAY THAT SOMETHING in the contents of this book inspired a change in you. Too often we overlook our shortcomings and focus on our husband's. If God changed our husband first, it would be almost impossible for us to change. God gave us the title *helpmeet,* which means "suitable, adapted, and complementary." We must be all of these things for our husband and for our children, who are extensions of our husband. How can we become suitable, adaptable, or complementary without being willing to change?

Be the example in your household of what happens when you totally submit to God and stay on the Potter's wheel. You will at some point reap what you have sown into your husband. Sit back and analyze your husband. Write down his behaviors that get your attention. If you sit and really think about those things you have listed, you can identify when you have sown that same behavior into him. The good news is you can turn it around by sowing good seed.

Treat your husband as you desire to be treated. First Peter 3:1–6 tells wives exactly how to win their husbands. Do your part. Sit back and watch God bring your marriage to the Ephesians 3:20 level: let God make your marriage grow exceedingly, abundantly, above all you could ask or think. This promise is contingent on the power that works in you. If you want better results, do better. No more excuses. Step up and be all that you can be. Be all that God has called you to be. Be all that your husband needs you to be. A positive change in you will result in the type of marriage God intended.

The process will start with you, woman of God!

To Contact the Author

inhisantg@yahoo.com